UP CLOSE

MUMMIES

KEVIN FLEURY

W
FRANKLIN WATTS
LONDON·SYDNEY

Published in 2007 by Franklin Watts

Copyright © 2007 Arcturus Publishing Limited

Franklin Watts
338 Euston Road
London NW1 3BH

Franklin Watts Australia
Level 17/207 Kent Street
Sydney, NSW 2000

Author: Kevin Fleury
Editor (new edition): Ella Fern
Designers (new edition): Steve West, Steve Flight

Picture credits: AKG/Erich Lessing: title page, 21 bottom; Ancient Art & Architecture: 11 top; The Ancient Egypt Picture Library: front cover, 5 bottom, 7 top; The Art Archive: 3, 4, back cover; CM Dixon: 12; Eurelios/Phillippe Plailly: 8 bottom, 11 bottom; Frank Spooner Picture Library: 7 bottom, 18 bottom, 21 top; Rex Features: 5 top, 9, 16 top; Robert Harding Picture Library: 13 top, bottom; Science Photo Library: 8 top, 14; The South American Picture Library: 2, 10, 18 top, 19, 23; Sygma: 6, 17, 20 top, bottom; Topham Picturepoint: 15; Werner Forman Archive: 16 bottom.

A CIP catalogue record for this book is available from the British Library

Dewey number: 393'.3

ISBN: 978-0-7496-7690-2

Printed in China

Franklin Watts is a division of Hachette Children's Books.

Contents

4 Meet the Mummies

6 The Mummies of Egypt

10 ¡Muchas Momias!

12 Pickled People of Europe

15 The Deep Freeze

17 All Dried Up

20 Modern Mummies

22 Glossary

23 Further Reading

24 Index

Meet The Mummies

Even though mummies are found all over the world, they are actually very rare. People die all the time, but not every dead body gets preserved—far from it! Normally, when a person dies, bacteria on the body cause it to decompose. Eventually just the skeleton is left behind. But sometimes, when conditions are just right and the bacteria can be stopped, the fleshy parts of the body are preserved—and a mummy is born!

ANCIENT ANIMALS
Mummies aren't limited to people! Ancient Egyptians mummified cats, dogs, birds, crocodiles, and even monkeys.

The ancient people of the Canary Islands also preserved their dead. The embalmers removed the internal organs and laid the body out in the sun to dry. Then they stuffed it with sand.

MUMMY MIA!
For centuries, Sicilian monks used chemicals including arsenic and milk of magnesia to preserve thousands of bodies.

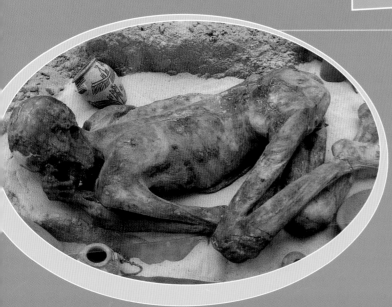

DESERT MUMMIES
The first Egyptian mummies were not Pharoahs in impressive tombs. They were just dead bodies buried in shallow graves in the desert, where the hot sand dried them out.

When the Egyptians realised that bodies buried in the hot desert sands were naturally preserved, they took it as a sign that the souls of their relatives were living in an afterlife. But a shallow hole in the desert wasn't regal enough for the Pharaohs. They wanted huge tombs, deep underground, to house their mummies.

NOSE JOB
Examination with X-rays revealed that the mummy makers stuffed Ramses' nose with peppercorns to help maintain its dignified shape.

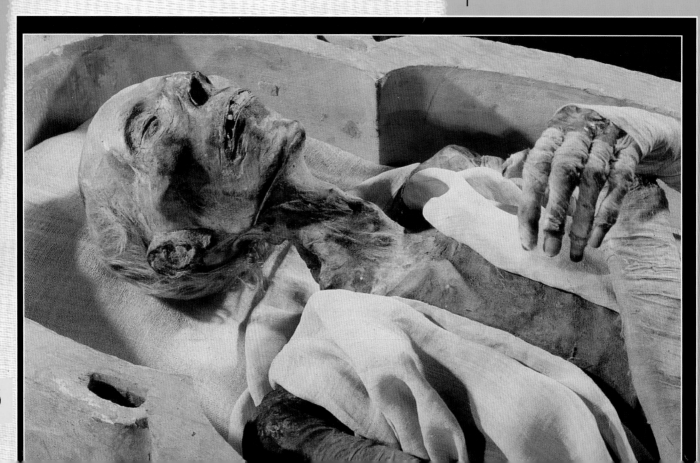

Egypt

NO BRAINER
Egyptian embalmers realized that organs began to decompose first. So they removed the stomach, intestines, liver, and lungs and dried them. They pulled the brain out through the nostrils.

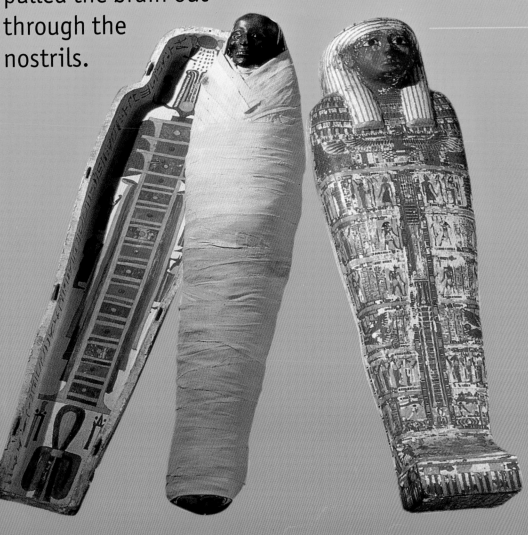

DRESSING
Each mummy was wrapped in layers of linen bandages and then fitted with a funeral mask. Finally, the mummy was placed into a coffin, often decorated to resemble the person inside.

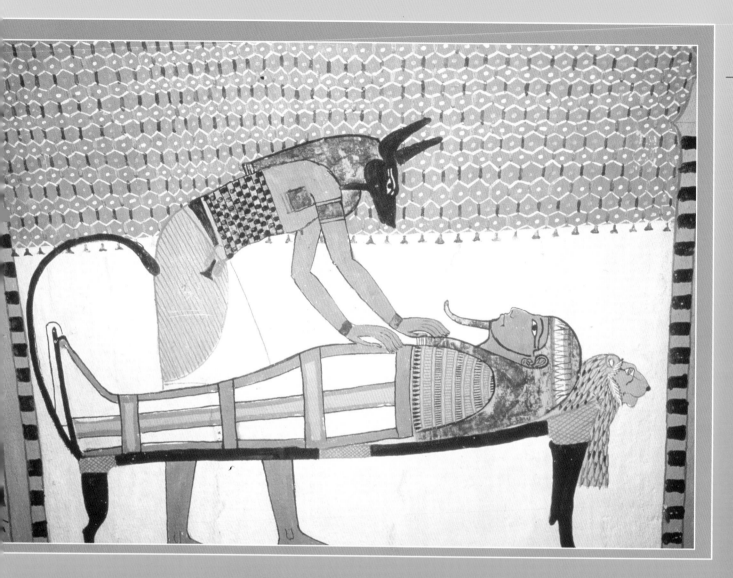

DISCOVERY

The greatest archeological discovery of the last several years was made by... a donkey! The donkey got its leg stuck in a small hole in the road, which was actually a crack in the ceiling of an underground tomb.

DEATH GOD

This picture shows Anubis, the Eygptian god of the dead, taking care of a mummy. Anubis was also the god of embalming, so it was his job to look after mummies all over the land.

A mummy spent its eternal afterlife in its tomb, so it needed to be prepared: food, clothes, and weapons were left for the soul to use.

CURSE?

After Howard Carter opened the tomb of the Pharaoh Tutankhamen in 1922, he suffered a run of bad luck. Many people blamed an ancient curse that protects the tomb from intruders...

If you've ever seen a real mummy in a museum, it probably came from Egypt. Although Egyptian mummies are the most famous, did you know that the Egyptians were not the first people to experiment with mummification? The Chinchorro people of South America began preserving their dead two thousand years before the Egyptians!

BASKET CASES

About 1,200 years ago, the people of the Atacama desert buried their dead in rope baskets. The heat and dryness of the desert preserved the bodies.

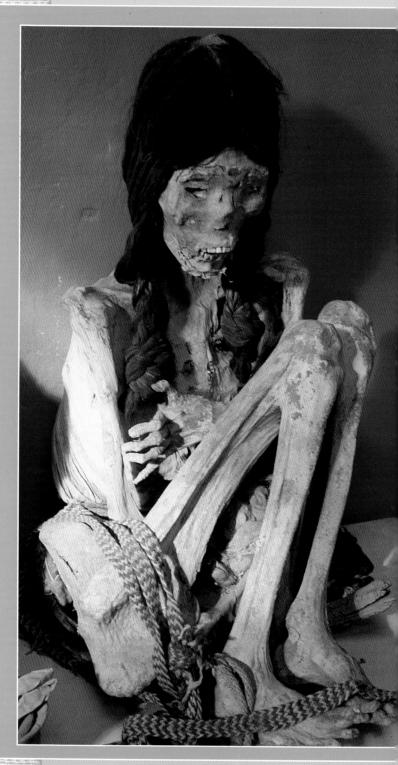

Momías!

The Incas used to sacrifice children on mountain summits as gifts to their gods. Five hundred years later, these bodies are still preserved due to the freezing, dry air of the mountaintops.

PRESERVED PERUVIANS
The early people of Peru often tied up their dead in a crouched position. Then they wrapped them in thick layers of beautifully embroidered cloth.

DITCH MUMMIES
While digging ditches to lay new water pipes, workers in Chile made a shocking discovery. Under just a few inches of sand lay an ancient Chinchorro cemetery of 96 mummies with masks placed over their faces.

11

Pickled People

J ust as cucumbers can be conserved in liquid by pickling, human bodies are sometimes preserved by the special conditions found in the water of a peat-moss bog. Throughout northern Europe, hundreds of bog bodies have been found. By studying these bodies, scientists can learn a lot about ancient religions and traditions.

LINDOW MAN
While cutting peat in Lindow Moss, England, in 1984, workers came upon a bog body. 2,300 years ago, Lindow man had been killed by a slit throat, smashed skull, and strangulation.

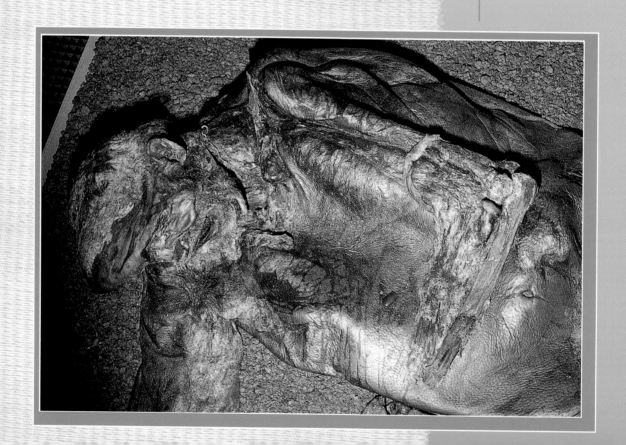

# of Europe

LAST MEAL
By studying the contents of this mummy's stomach, scientists discovered that his last meal was vegetable soup!

TEENS, TOO
A 14-year-old female bog body found in Germany was blindfolded with a coloured cloth. Like other bog bodies, she was killed as a sacrifice.

REST IN PEACE
Tollund Man was found in Danish bog in 1950. He was between 30 and 40 years of age when he was killed by hanging. Despite this, the expression on his face is peaceful.

The Deep Freeze

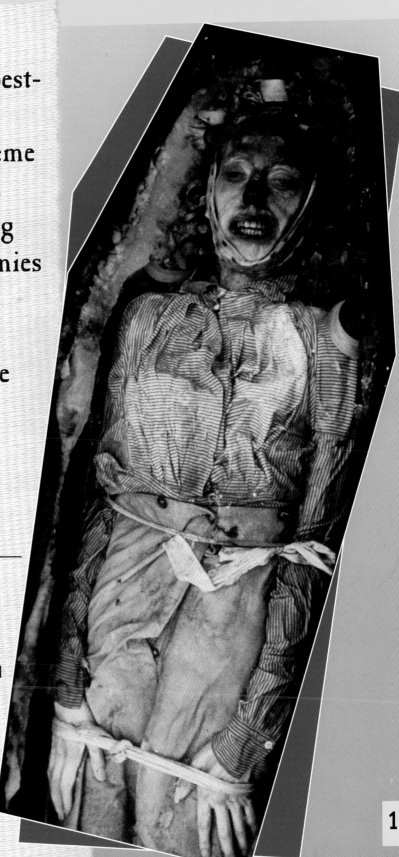

S ome of the oldest and best-preserved mummies are formed accidentally by extreme cold—freezing temperatures prevent bacteria from causing decay. Sometimes ice mummies are preserved even better by becoming freeze-dried. This happens when conditions are dry and windy as well as extremely cold.

COLD VOYAGE

150 years ago, a ship went missing in the Arctic. Search parties later discovered three graves on an Arctic island and inside they found the ice mummies of three crew members.

15

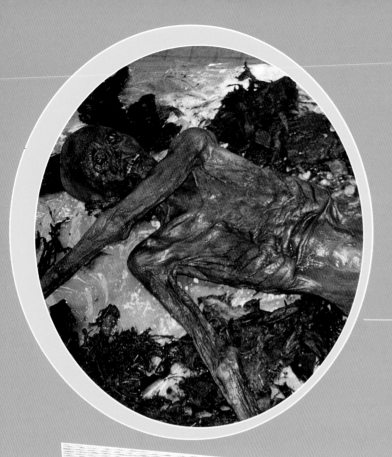

ICE MAN

The Ice Man is the oldest well-preserved human mummy in the world. How old? About 5,300 years!

Small marks on the Ice Man's body suggest that he had received acupuncture treatments for back pain.

ESKIMO MUMMIES

In 1972, hunters in Greenland found the freeze-dried mummies of eight Inuit women and children. They were aged between 6 months and 50 years old. The bodies were stacked on top of each other.

ICY TOMB

In 1993, archeologists in Siberia discovered the tomb of a woman who lived more than 2,000 years ago. Her tomb was filled with ice because water had leaked into it and frozen!

All Dried Up & No Place to Go

T he most common way that mummies are created is by rapid drying. The climate may preserve a body if it is especially hot, dry, or both. Some mummies are created when exposed to moisture-absorbing substances, like salt. Other mummies are created by drying with hot smoke, just like beef jerky! However, if water gets near a dried mummy, then it quickly starts to decompose.

PRETTY WOMAN
Discovered in 1980 in the Taklimakan Desert, the Beauty of Loulan died around 1800 B.C.

MUMMY MUSEUM

In Guanajuato, Mexico, people were dug up and put on display in El Museo de las Momias (The Museum of the Mummies) unless their relatives paid up!

In Papua New Guinea, people used to hang their dead relatives in the trees to dry in the hot sun.

MYSTERIOUS

More than 100 mummies of up to 4,000 years old were found in China's Taklimakan Desert. But strangely, they look far more European than Chinese! So where did these mystery mummies come from, and how did they end up in China?

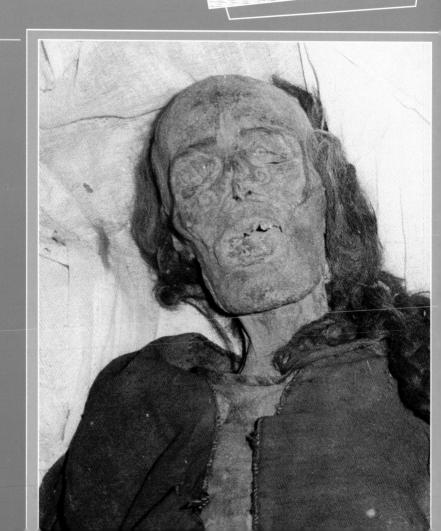

DO-IT-YOURSELF

Some Buddhist priests in Japan used to practice a bizarre form of mummification—on themselves! Surrounded by huge candles, they starved themselves to death. The heat of the burning candles preserved them.

DISTRESS

These mummies were discovered at a ceremonial site in the Andes mountains. They were probably the victims of ritual sacrifice. From the expressions on their faces, it looks as though they were in pain when they died.

Modern Mummies

S ome mummies were created within the last century... and some are still being made today! Like their ancient counterparts, these modern mummies also cheat death. By sticking around, they serve as a constant reminder and live on in our memories.

DOMESTIC MUMMIES
Unwilling to say good-bye to their pets, some people are choosing to have them mummified instead!

WRAPPING
One company mummifies humans by wrapping them in bandages, like the ancient Egyptians.

Some people think that Walt Disney's head is frozen and buried in Disneyland, but Disney was cremated in 1966.

BIG CHILL

Faced with terminal illness, some people have had their bodies frozen in liquid nitrogen. They hope to be thawed in the future when the cure for their fatal disease is found. This practice is called cryonics.

MUMMY OF MOSCOW

The mummified body of Vladimir Lenin, the founder of the Soviet state, is on display in Moscow. Lenin looks so good that some people insist the body must be a wax dummy.

Glossary

Acupuncture
Ancient Chinese treatment using needles.

Archeologist
Someone who studies the remains and relics of ancient sites.

Arctic
The Arctic is the cold, icy land around the North Pole.

Bacteria
Tiny cells that can cause disease, but also help with processes such as digestion and decomposition.

Cryonics
Freezing a dead body to preserve it for the future.

Embalmer
Someone who treats dead bodies to prevent them from decomposing.

Howard Carter (1874–1939)
A British Egyptologist (person who studies Ancient Egypt) who discovered the tomb of Tutenkhamen in 1922.

Inuit people
Eskimos from North America or Greenland.

Mummification
The process by which a dead body becomes a mummy, eg. by freezing or drying out.

Peat bog
Decomposing plants that form a mushy, wet area of ground.

Pharaoh
A king of ancient Egypt.

Strangulation
To strangle somebody, or to kill them by stopping air going down the windpipe.

Vladimir Lenin (1870–1924)
A Russian revolutionary and the first leader of the Soviet state in Russia.

Further Reading

The Mystery of the Egyptian Mummy
Joyce Filer, Oxford University Press, 2003

Ancient Egypt
Peter Chrisp, Dorling Kindersley
(Revealed series), 2002

Encyclopedia of Ancient Egypt
Gill Harvey and Struan Reid, Usborne,
2002

Make this Egyptian Mummy
Iain Ashman, Usborne (Make this Model
series), 2002

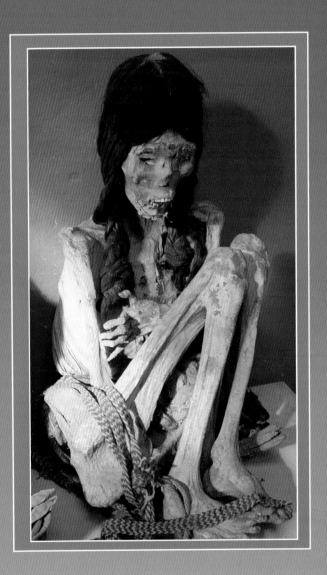

Index

A
acupuncture *16, 22*
afterlife *6, 9*
Andes *19*
animals *4, 20*
Anubis *9*
archeologists *16, 22*
Arctic *15, 22*
Atacama Desert *10*

B
bacteria *4, 15, 22*
bandages *7, 20*
Beauty of Loulan *17*
bogs *12–14, 22*

C
Canary Islands *5*
Carter, Howard *9, 22*
cemeteries *11*
chemicals *5*
Chile *11*
China *18*
cryonics *21, 22*

D
decomposition *4, 7, 17*
dried mummies *5, 10, 17–19*

E
Egyptian mummies *4, 5, 6–9, 10*
embalmers *5, 7, 22*
England *12*
Eskimo mummies *16*

F
frozen mummies *15–16, 21*

G
Germany *13*
graves *5, 15*
Greenland *16*

I
ice *15, 16*
Ice Man *16*
Inca mummies *11*

J
Japan *19*

L
Lenin, Vladimir *21, 22*
Lindow Moss *12*

M
masks *7, 11*
Mexico *18*
Museum of the Mummies *18*

O
organs *5, 7*

P
Papua New Guinea *18*
Peru *11*
Pharaohs *6, 9, 22*

R
Ramses the Great *6*

S
sacrifice *11, 13, 19*
scientists *12, 13*
Siberia *16*
Sicilian mummies *5*
skeleton *4*
souls *6, 9*
South America *10*
starvation *19*

T
Tollund man *14*
tombs *5, 6, 8, 9, 16*
Tutankhamen *9*

W
Walt Disney *20*

X
X-rays *6*

Toot & Puddle

I'll Be Home for Christmas

by
Holly Hobbie

WALKER BOOKS
AND SUBSIDIARIES
LONDON · BOSTON · SYDNEY · AUCKLAND

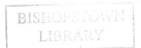

First published 2001 by Little, Brown and Company, USA

First published in Great Britain 2003 by Walker Books Ltd, 87 Vauxhall Walk, London SE11 5HJ

2 4 6 8 10 9 7 5 3 1

Copyright © 2001 by Holly Hobbie and Douglas Hobbie

The right of Holly Hobbie to be identified as author/illustrator of this work has been asserted by her in accordance with the Copyright, Designs and Patents Act 1988

This book has been typeset in Optima, Windsor Light and Poetica

Printed in Singapore

British Library Cataloguing in Publication Data:
a catalogue record for this book is available from the British Library

ISBN 1-84428-001-2

www.walkerbooks.co.uk

Central Adult:
Douglas: 492
St Mary's Rd

To Hope

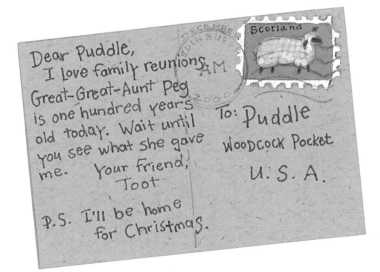

Dear Puddle,
  I love family reunions.
Great-Great-Aunt Peg
is one hundred years
old today. Wait until
you see what she gave
me.   Your Friend,
         Toot

P.S. I'll be home
     for Christmas.

Scotland

DECEMBER
EDINBURGH
AM
2000

To: Puddle
WOODCOCK Pocket
  U.S.A.

"My dear Toot," said the ancient aunt, "this is for you. It is my lucky nut!"

Back in Woodcock Pocket, Puddle couldn't wait for
Toot any longer. Christmas was only a few days away.
And there was everything to do.

Puddle signed all the cards Merry Christmas! and Puddle
He would have to wait until Toot returned before he could mail them.

To: puddle@woodcockpocket.com
Subject: Christmas

Puds,

Edinburgh is having a snowstorm. All
flights delayed. But don't decorate the
tree without me. I'm on my way
home...somehow.

Your pal,

Toot

P.S. I'm full of Christmas spirit.

Meanwhile …
at Woodcock Pocket

"Fruitcake is one of Toot's favourite things," said Puddle.

"How many do you think we need?" Tulip asked.

Christmas Eve was only one day away.
"How can Toot possibly get home in time?" Puddle said.
"He has to," said Tulip.

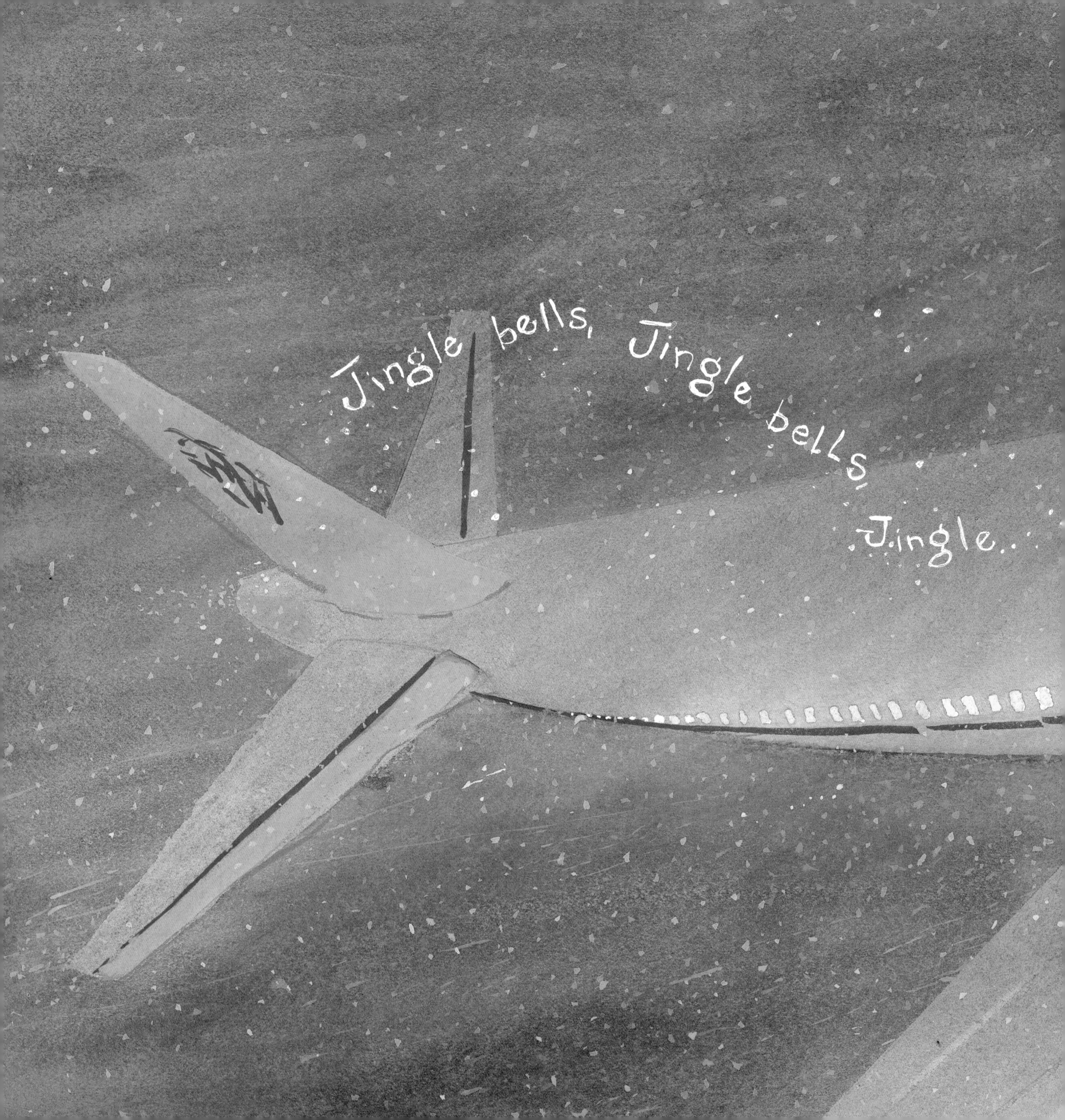
Jingle bells, Jingle bells, Jingle..

...all...the way...

WIDE WORLD AIRWAYS

When Toot finally arrived in Boston, it was snowing and very late.
Everything had come to a stop, even trains and buses and taxicabs.
I promised Puddle I'd be home tonight, Toot thought.

Toot hiked far from the city. The night was cold and the snow was deep. He trudged on until, at last, he could go no further.

Toot hugged himself to keep warm. There in his pocket he felt the lucky nut. He'd forgotten all about that special gift. *It's Christmas Eve,* he thought. *I wish I was home in Woodcock Pocket.*

"It's snowing so hard," Puddle said.
"It's beautiful," said Tulip.

"If only Toot were here."

Toot was startled by a tinkling, jingling sound.
As he peered into the dark, he saw a faint light coming
toward him. It twinkled and flickered in the snowy night.

"Where are you headed, laddie?"

"Woodcock Pocket," said Toot. "It's miles and miles from here."

"Climb aboard," the driver said. "I know the way."

The first snowfall had turned Woodcock Pocket into a sparkling wonderland. Everything was ready. Everything was perfect.
But where was his friend?

Then…
"I'm home!"
"You are! You're finally here!"

Toot told his friends of his adventure and how he finally got
back to Woodcock Pocket.
"I loved the sleigh ride," he said. "It felt like we were flying."
"I wonder who that driver was," said Puddle.

"Let's hang this on the tree," said Toot.
"What is that?" Tulip asked.
"It's beautiful," said Puddle.
"This is Great-Great-Aunt Peg's lucky nut," Toot told them.

It wasn't easy to fall asleep on Christmas Eve.

"Toot," Puddle said, "do you hear a jingling sound?"

Toot listened. "Maybe."

"I think I definitely hear something," said Puddle.

"Then I think we'd better go to sleep," Toot said. "Right away."

Puddle agreed. "I'll count to twenty."

But before Puddle counted to ten, he and his friend were fast asleep.

When they wake up, it will be Christmas.